GW00599519

The Aquarius Woman

The Aq

Ariel Books

**Andrews McMeel
Publishing**

Kansas City

uarius
Woman

January 21–February 19

Julie Mars

Illustrated by Sarah Hollander

ISBN: 0-7407-1427-9
Library of Congress Catalog Card Number: 00-106911

designed by Junie Lee
typeset by Ellen M. Carnahan

Contents

Introduction

Did you ever wish upon a star? Have you ever studied the night sky, transfixed by its vast beauty and magnificent mystery?

Astrologers believe that the celestial bodies overhead correspond in some significant way with our own bodies (and personalities) here on Earth.

For more than five thousand years, women have gazed heavenward, searching for connections between the cosmos and their own human minds and spirits. Looking to the planets and stars for guidance in the areas of romance and friendship gives all women a powerful way to understand and better direct their own lives and personal destinies.

PLANETARY RULERS

Astrology is the product of centuries of precise observation of both the planets and human nature, yet it also incorporates a degree of intuition. So when an astrologer identifies a sun sign, it is much more than a convenient label. It is a strong indicator of the particular cosmic energy that helps shape each woman's personality. There even tends to be a natural affinity between two people born under the same planetary ruler.

Aries (March 21–April 20) is ruled by Mars, the planet of forcefulness, physical energy, and sex drive.

Taurus (April 21–May 21), like Libra, is ruled by Venus, the planet of love, affection, and pleasure.

Gemini (May 22–June 21), like Virgo, is ruled by Mercury, the planet of communication and travel.

Cancer (June 22–July 23) is ruled by the Moon, the planet of reflection, cyclical change, and receptivity.

Leo (July 24–August 23) is ruled by the Sun, the planet of self-centeredness, brilliance, and warmth.

Virgo (August 24–September 23), like Gemini, is ruled by Mercury, the planet of communication and travel.

Libra (September 24–October 23), like Taurus, is ruled by Venus, the planet of love, affection, and pleasure.

Scorpio (October 24–November 22) is ruled by Pluto, the planet of transformation through the powers of both creativity and destruction.

Sagittarius (November 23–December 21) is ruled by Jupiter, the planet of good luck, generosity, and success.

Capricorn (December 22–January 20) is ruled by Saturn, the planet of hard work, responsibility, and endurance.

Aquarius (January 21–February 19) is ruled by Uranus, the planet of originality, change, and sudden inspiration.

Pisces (February 20–March 20) is ruled by Neptune, the planet of illusion, mystery, and the force of imagination.

ELEMENTS AND QUALITIES

Two other basic concepts are essential to astrological interpretation. The first is called the *element*, of which there are four: *earth, air, fire,* and *water.* Each element carries with it a vast body of associations that help you to understand how your sign interacts with other signs.

Earth. This element is often connected with such traits as steadiness, practicality, and predictability. "Earthy" women tend to be firmly rooted and notoriously stable. The three earth signs are Taurus, Virgo, and Capricorn.

Air. The signs associated with this element are more likely to be intellectual and analytical. "Airy" women tend to display great emotional detachment and are often described as elusive or unavailable. Gemini, Libra, and Aquarius are the three air signs.

Fire. This element is associated with activity, energy, and impulsiveness. "Fiery" women tend to be vivacious, dynamic, optimistic, and domineering. Aries, Leo, and Sagittarius comprise the three fire signs.

Water. This element is often associated with emotion and intuition. The water signs are Cancer, Scorpio, and Pisces. "Watery" women tend to be moody, sensitive, creative, and deep.

The final astrological variable is the *quality* of a particular sign. The quality reflects a sun sign's relationship to the rest of the world. There are three qualities: *cardinal,* which initiates change; *mutable,* which adapts to circumstances; and *fixed,* which maintains the status quo. Aries, Cancer, Libra, and Capricorn are outgoing, energetic cardinal signs. Taurus, Leo, Scorpio, and Aquarius are fixed, or resistant. Gemini, Virgo, Sagittarius, and Pisces are flexible, or mutable.

Each sign is a unique combination of quality and element. Because of this specificity, women can glean much personal information from even a minor astrological analysis. The complex art of astrology, with its mix of science and subjectivity, offers all women insight into the present...and a hint or two about the future!

Just the Facts on Aquarius

Motto:	"I know"
Element:	Air
Quality:	Fixed
Opposite Sign:	Leo
Ruling Planet:	Uranus
Animal:	Birds
Jewel:	Amethyst
Numbers:	One and seven

AQUARIUS

Innovative, independent, and open-minded, the typical Aquarius woman is perhaps the most unconventional female in the zodiac—and she's proud of it! She's usually content to go her merry way without so much as a backward glance at rules, regulations, and the expectations of others. Because of her individuality, though, she is sometimes criticized by those with more rigid agendas—or more narrow minds.

Could she possibly have avoided such a progressive but quirky path? With Uranus as her ruling planet, it's not likely. Uranus creates an affinity for change, the unexpected, and the original—and the typical Aquarian woman embodies this to the fullest. Yet her nature is also fixed—which means she's determined, persistent, and *very* opinionated.

This paradoxical mix of adaptability and inflexibility is often confusing to others—especially significant others—but once they realize that ideas and principles are precious to the Water Bearer, while status and material possessions are not, they will be better able to predict her areas of absolute stubbornness. Remember, "I know" is her motto.

An air sign, the Aquarian woman is born to communicate, and the intellect is her terrain of choice. She tends to be somewhat detached emotionally, though she is known for her skill with people of all types. She thoroughly enjoys an active, varied social life and is exceptionally beloved by and tolerant of others.

Often called the zodiac's Great Humanitarian, the Water Bearer is typically concerned with social issues related to fairness and equality. This is because she is on a quest for meaning—in her relationships, her work, and her daily life.

The typical Aquarian woman dreads boredom and will often go to great lengths to find adventure. Others tend to find it an adventure just to be with her, for the Water Bearer is a true original.

Aquarius and Friends

Aquarius Woman/Aries Friends

Sparks of friendship ignite a high-spirited but deep bond. These two egg each other on to excitement, unorthodox fun…and (hopefully) harmless mischief.

Aquarius Woman/Taurus Friends

The Taurean sense of humor inspires the Aquarian woman—and vice versa. These easygoing pals will last—if each sidesteps the other's dogmatic tendencies.

Aquarius Woman / Gemini Friends

High spirits, sharp minds, and great wit make daily life a laugh a minute. Aquarius and Gemini may not be concerned with practical matters, but do they care? Definitely not!

Aquarius Woman / Cancer Friends

Both are somewhat unpredictable, which keeps this friendship interesting. But Cancer must not make too many demands, or the independent Water Bearer will quickly fly away.

Aquarius Woman/Leo Friends

Both have the energy and the enthusiasm to build a glorious friendship—but Aquarius should leave Leo out of her humanitarian ventures. The Lion just isn't interested!

Aquarius Woman/Virgo Friends

Interesting conversation and passionate debate—these await the Aquarius/Virgo friendship. As long as they give each other some room, these two can be great pals.

Aquarius Woman / Libra Friends

The friendly chemistry is immediately apparent. Intellectual fun and games and a shared devotion to art and entertainment make this air/air friendship one of a kind!

Aquarius Woman / Scorpio Friends

Aquarius may feel both intrigued by and suspicious of her Scorpio pals. But as long as she maintains her own borders, she can codirect this supercharged friendship.

Aquarius Woman/Sagittarius Friends

The Water Bearer is beloved for her openhearted friendliness, and the Archer is universally acknowledged as the best friend of the zodiac. This match is made in the stars.

Aquarius Woman/Capricorn Friends

Goats may seem a bit stern, and the Water Bearer seems unnecessarily eccentric. In small doses, though, they may enjoy each other. But don't mix finance and friendship.

Aquarius Woman / Aquarius Friends

Social, independent, and charmingly eccentric, the Aquarian woman thrives with other Aquarians. In fact, the more, the merrier. And their friendships are merry, indeed.

Aquarius Woman / Pisces Friends

The Water Bearer is drawn to the Fish, and vice versa. Call it a philosophical affinity or a mutual admiration society. These two often become the best of pals.

The Aquarius Woman in Love

Deeply interested in the opposite sex, more than a little flirtatious, and vivacious to the max, the Aquarius woman is a front-runner in the game of love. Her magnetic mix of brains and charm creates an intriguing aura that many suitors respond to.

But the Water Bearer can also be elusive and emotionally aloof. She's more interested in the mind (and a strong intellectual rapport) than in romantic games and glamour. And she's adamant about her privacy and her independence, so any potential partner will need to give her space—and take a lot of his own!

Once she's hooked, though, she's loyal and loving. And she can be relied on to keep the romance fresh and new, no matter how long it lasts. She simply wouldn't have it any other way!

Aquarius Woman/ Aries Man

The typical Aquarian woman's first rules of love are simple: Don't try to tie her down, boss her around, or cage her up. If her potential partner accepts that, the romantic negotiations—and the fun— can begin! And the Aries man not only accepts it, he applauds. When the Water Bearer hears his approval, she usually breathes a sigh of romantic relief.

Why? Because she recognizes a kindred spirit. He may be a fire sign, but the Aquarius woman has no problem with that; in fact, she likes it! Fire and air are a thoroughly combustible combination, and as far as she's concerned, the more fireworks, the better.

With her abundance of tolerance, the female Water Bearer is likely to understand the Ram's need to lead. She'll certainly find creative ways to cope with it, at any rate. It may even be something of a trade-off: She steps back occasionally and follows, but in exchange she reaps exuberance, intensity, and brilliance.

And let's not forget the passion. The Aquarian woman tends to live in her head, but the Ram stands a better chance than most of bringing her out of the clouds and into her body. With their shared adventurous spirit and impulsiveness, a world of intimate fun awaits this Aquarius/Aries match. And neither of them will spiral into fits of jealousy or depression if the other needs to take a little time off periodically. After all, intensity is fun, but it's also exhausting!

If the Ram wants to hold on to his Water Bearer (and he usually does), he must learn to be a bit less verbally blunt and a bit more tuned in to her needs. If the Aquarian woman wants to keep her Aries man from running off, she should try to be less dogmatic and argumentative.

But problems usually go up in smoke, and the romance can smolder eternally for the Aquarian woman and her Aries mate.

Aquarius Woman/
Taurus Man

Meditate for a moment on the difference between air and earth. The air is free and easy and whimsical. The earth is solid, immovable, and permanent. In astrological terms, air is intellectual and communicative; earth is practical and stable. Air is given to analysis and conversation; earth, to hard work and dependability.

The point is that there are some basic differences in orientation between the

Aquarian woman and the Taurean man. She likes to fly, while he wants deep roots. She thrives on change; he tends to resent it. She is typically a bit careless—with cash and her romantic obligations. He is often conservative and cautious—particularly with his heart. And both are fixed signs, so stubbornness, strong opinions, and various forms of inflexibility are to be expected.

The romantic prognosis isn't especially promising...yet a surprising number of Aquarius/Taurus couples beat the odds and find true happiness together.

These lovers are able to overcome some formidable obstacles—his possessiveness, her eccentricity, his temper, her distance—with grace and style. It's simply a matter of choice … and vigilance.

In this match, the Aquarius woman has an opportunity to explore the realm of deep, satisfying sensuality. It won't hurt her to come down to Earth for a visit from time to time! And the Bull can lighten up under the Aquarius influence—something he can benefit from, especially when he starts his snorting, foot-stomping routine.

Both have the stability to make a romantic decision and stick to it. The Water Bearer and the Bull who find themselves emotionally enmeshed should focus on their mutual affection, and on the simple fact that opposites attract. With patience, that attraction can blossom into a garden of true love.

Aquarius Woman/ Gemini Man

Put the airy Water Bearer together with the airy Twins, and they will *all* take off on a passing breeze. And there won't be any looking back or worrying about where they might end up. This love match is typically full of adventure and surprise, but it has enormous stability too, the stability that comes from trust.

Perhaps it tends to work so well because the Aquarian woman and the

Gemini man truly understand each other. Both are intellectually oriented and thrive in romance when the communication is clear, concise, and constant. Such verbal intensity might wear others out, but not these two. Each was born with an unlimited vocabulary and words to spare!

Since both the female Water Bearer and the Twins are people oriented, they easily fly together from one intriguing social scene to the next with energy and enthusiasm. True, the Aquarius woman is typically more interested in humanitarian issues than her Gemini mate, but she also tends to be tolerant of his perhaps more superficial curiosity—and where it leads them. Both are drawn to offbeat places (and people), and life in the fast lane suits them fine.

The Water Bearer is very susceptible to the Twins' inherent charm—and his sexiness. He, in turn, is drawn to her detached independence. Both of them typically require that the ties that bind be very loose, but neither the Aquarius woman nor the Gemini man is afraid of permanent commitment if the chemistry is right.

And between the Aquarius woman and the Gemini man, the chemistry often is right. When they fly away together, a love that's based more on friendship than on passion can form—and grow, and grow. Romantic turbulence may toss them around at times, but it won't usually blow them apart.

Aquarius Woman/
Cancer Man

What happens when an energetic, altru-
istic Aquarian woman meets a Cancerian
daydreamer? Do they combine their
imagination and ideals and set about to
right all the wrongs of society? Are they
likely to form a committee of two that
fights for humanitarian causes by day and
explores each other by night?

It might seem so in the very beginning, but the bad news is that this tends

to be a difficult match over the long run. And many of the problems can be traced to one essential difference: independence versus attachment. The typical Aquarian female is militantly independent. She is born with a deep desire for freedom—and it shows in her free spirit, her free thinking, and her live-and-let-live attitude.

The Cancerian man, by comparison, tends to be insecure and somewhat clinging. The Crab thrives in an intimate relationship and tends to become snappish and cranky when his desire to stay home and cuddle (every night) is not met with enthusiasm by his independent mate.

The Aquarian woman often dreads having to spend extended periods within the four walls of home. When she is cooped up too long, she becomes argumentative—and she'll likely hurt the Crab's vulnerable feelings. When he withdraws into his shell, she takes refuge in a cool objectivity that can become quite inflexible. The emotional route back to each other is not very well marked.

Because the Cancerian man in love is typically possessive and restrictive, the

Aquarian woman often feels pressured to conform. This is not generally a realistic option. The female Water Bearer enjoys a little harmless flirtation; the Crab becomes moody and sulky if he momentarily doubts her loyalty.

In romance and in life, she typically thrives on experimentation. He needs security. Need we say more?

Aquarius Woman/
Leo Man

When the fiery Leo man steps into the spotlight and begins to beam, the typical Aquarius woman is bound to take notice. She is powerfully drawn to his nobility and his expansive, enthusiastic personality. She enjoys the Lion's self-assurance and natural wit. And his general flamboyance—something she herself lacks— is enormously appealing.

The moment the Lion focuses on the

Water Bearer, he is likely to be just as impressed. She's brainy, quirky, and casually elegant. She's sexy, amusing, and just emotionally aloof enough to keep him on his romantic toes. And the Aquarius woman is independent and easygoing, so the Leo man knows it's unlikely that she'll cramp his style.

This air/fire match provides both the heat (his) and the imagination (hers) to ignite a hot romance. But remember, Aquarius and Leo are astrological opposites, so both an initial attraction and subterranean tensions can be expected.

One possible romantic land mine is the Lion's determination to lead. With the Sun as his ruling planet, he simply expects the world to orbit around him. And his motto, "I will," is a dead giveaway—he isn't likely to take "no" for an answer.

The Aquarius woman, by contrast, is more interested in saving the world, questing for knowledge, and being a friend to all, than she is in providing the starstruck audience that Leo requires. And she's not about to be led by anyone—particularly her significant other. Her Lion mate is likely to be miffed—and later, he may even feel sorely neglected.

The Water Bearer and Leo the Lion are advised to take their problems to the bedroom and work them out in private. With their air/fire passion, they stand a good chance of resolving romantic conflict.

Aquarius Woman/ Virgo Man

It's a mental world for the typical Aquarius woman. She's most likely to find peace and happiness when her mind is thoroughly engaged. Intellectual exploration, rationality, objectivity, and detachment—these are the tools with which she builds her mental empire.

Enter the Virgo man. His motto is "I analyze," and nothing may please him more than a search for truth—as long as it's grounded in fact. He conscientiously works to improve himself, and perfection is his ultimate goal.

It's very possible that the female Water Bearer and the male Virgin will take their precious common mental ground and create a romantic empire. A meeting of the minds is a powerful aphrodisiac for both.

But this love match should expect some problem areas. The Virgo man likes everything in its proper place, while the Aquarius woman tends be careless—even with her affection. She tends to sidestep rules and regulations, while the Virgin adheres to them religiously and is likely to make up a few of his own.

Then there's the social world. The Water Bearer thrives among an interesting (and preferably odd) assortment of pals. The Virgin would typically prefer to forge a few deep human bonds—and ignore the rest of the folks on the planet.

Aquarius is a fixed sign, thus the female Water Bearer is often opinionated and stubborn. Should her Virgo partner criticize her for this (and he will), the relationship may unravel. Wise Virgins will hold their critical tongues and enjoy the rest of the ride with the Water Bearer.

And the Aquarius woman must understand that there is beauty in order—and work a bit harder to integrate it into her life. With a little compromise on both sides, this love can reach the Aquarian sky and still stay firmly rooted in the Virgin earth!

Aquarius Woman/
Libra Man

There's a certain magic that happens when two signs that share a common element meet. This is perhaps particularly true of air signs. Since they tend to require lightness, detachment, and a breezy approach to life, it's easy for them to recognize each other—and once they do, they're likely to take off together for parts unknown.

Consider the Aquarius woman and the Libra man. Both are supremely interested in other people, the arts, and abstract concepts such as fairness and equality. It's the most natural thing in the world that they would run into each other socially. And since both the Water Bearer and the Scales are charming and amusing, a mutual attraction is quite the norm.

The Aquarius/Libra match is the kind of attraction that usually lasts. Each can be counted on to breathe new life into the romance whenever it begins to seem dull or routine. Why? Because neither can stand it when the excitement begins to fade.

Though they're both air signs, there are just enough differences to keep it intriguing. The Libra man, for example, is typically much more sensuous than the Aquarius woman—so he can show her the ropes of physical pleasure. And she is more idealistic and humanitarian than he is, so she may lure the Scales into rewarding projects in which his diplomacy and tact are valued.

And speaking of diplomacy, the Libra man is one of the few men in the zodiac who is able to handle the Water Bearer's quirky obstinace. She knows this—and appreciates it. The Aquarius woman may even learn to relax her rigidity now and then, just to keep the peace at home.

This is typically a love duet that requires a light touch. It's a perfect combination if the Aquarian's heart's desire is to find a partner and maintain her precious independence too.

Aquarius Woman/ Scorpio Man

The Water Bearer is typically attracted to oddballs and eccentrics. Remember, it's part of her Aquarian heritage to be tolerant of (and charmed by) quirkiness. And the Scorpio man, with his powerful sexual magnetism, mystery, and intensity, may very well capture her heart.

But be warned! This is not an easy romantic match! True, it may be passionate. And true, the Scorpion and the Water

Bearer may become emotionally enmeshed before good sense asserts itself. Should this happen, the best advice to both is to buckle up and prepare for a bumpy ride!

Let's face it: How can an Aquarian free spirit ever satisfy the superpossessive Scorpio man? And how will he, a man who prizes the predictable in love, find happiness with the Water Bearer, who's universally known (as well as frequently loved) for her elusive and romantically unorthodox ways?

Not to mention the fact that both are

fixed signs, so compromise is often difficult, or the fact that words like *obstinate*, *unyielding*, and *dogmatic* are frequently used to describe both the Water Bearer and the Scorpion. A workable romance requires flexibility—which the Aquarian woman can develop, but she fears that with the Scorpio man, the "give" will usually be hers and the "take," his.

On the other hand, both are known for idealism and an interest in philosophy. Both are charismatic and creative. And rules are made to be broken—particularly by the Aquarius woman.

She enjoys a risk—and the payoff could be a very grand passion.

In the game of life—and love—forewarned is forearmed. But in this case, both the Aquarius woman and the Scorpio man should drop their arms and simply surrender to each other. If they resist this mutual romantic capitulation, the road may be very rough indeed.

Aquarius Woman/ Sagittarius Man

Begin with one free-spirited Aquarian woman. Add a footloose, restless Sagittarius man . . . and the result could be pure romantic happiness. This is truly a love match of two kindred souls.

Of course, she's more idealistic and desirous of helping others than he is. And he's less likely to finish what he begins than she is. But aside from those relatively minor obstacles, there's nothing but blue skies and clear sailing ahead for the Water Bearer and the Archer who happen to fall in love.

Consider the basic romantic equation. Ruled by Jupiter, the planet of expansion and abundance, the Archer is cheerful, optimistic, and ebullient. What better soul mate for the Aquarian woman? Both of them tend to be cerebral rather than physical, both dread boredom and thrive on excitement, and both may preach an easygoing, live-and-let-live lifestyle—and practice it in daily life too.

Best of all, neither is typically jealous.

So when the Aquarian woman needs to spread her wings and fly solo for a while, the Archer will happily step out of her way. And should the fiery Sagittarius man feel a burning desire to cut loose, his Aquarian mate is likely to wish him well and continue on her own merry way without so much as a romantic doubt about his fidelity—and that's only if she happens to care about that!

Of course, there will be some trouble spots: The Archer can be outspoken and bossy; the female Water Bearer can become a fixed-sign bulldozer at times.

Each may unthinkingly trample on the other's feelings.

And neither of them is very commitment oriented—at least, in the beginning. But once they both come to realize that freedom and commitment can actually coexist in their case, they may form a love bond that lasts ... and lasts.

Aquarius Woman/
Capricorn Man

This is the story of an earthbound Capricorn man and an airy Aquarius female. He may see her pass by and wonder if he can convince her to descend into his earthy realm...because it's not likely that he'll be able to ascend into hers. She may catch sight of him down there, solid and steadfast, and momentarily entertain the idea of voluntarily clipping her own wings—just to alight next to him.

But the initial infatuation probably won't last, because this is a particularly tempestuous air/earth match. The odds are not in its favor, and in this case, it's hard to beat them! The Capricorn man's ruling planet, Saturn, inspires a sense of discipline, constraint, and limitation, while the Aquarius woman's planet, Uranus, rules the realms of unexpectedness and change. And both tend to be devoted to their respective cosmic force fields!

When it comes to the all important issue of money, the Water Bearer and the

Goat couldn't be further apart. She likes to keep it flowing, in and out, in and out, like the water in her zodiacal jug. He wants to keep it, bury it, and wait for it to grow. Both are bound to experience frustration with the other's spending habits—and neither is likely to change. So, at the very least, separate checking accounts are probably a must, and the Goat might be well served to develop a blind eye regarding her extravagance. But it won't be easy.

Of course, the Capricorn man could lighten up under the Aquarian woman's influence, and the Water Bearer could stand to be a bit more prudent, like the Goat. But the big secret is that neither really wants to learn the lessons the other has to teach. And with this kind of resistance, romance is tricky.

Some couples beat the odds. And some of them are Aquarius/Capricorn pairs. Good luck!

Aquarius Woman/ Aquarius Man

Two peas in a pod—that's the typical relationship between an Aquarius woman and man. Not only are they comfortable and cozy together, they genuinely like each other. And should this basic affection blossom into true love, the transition will typically be smooth and seamless.

And why not? Both tend to be somewhat enthralled with their astrological heritage—so it's a short step to falling in love with each other! They share idealism, a great sense of humor, and a passion for freedom and independence. They genuinely understand each other's emotional detachment, and rarely find themselves in the messy romantic fits of jealousy that often plague other relationships. They're simply custom-made for each other!

Because both tend to be innovative and original, the creativity in this Aquarius/Aquarius match knows no bounds. That applies to general life—and to the romantic realm too. Their love connection often sizzles with adventure. Notice we did not say "passion." What this match tends to lack in physical fervor, it more than makes up in inventive intellectual intimacy. Try it! It's out of this world, as two Aquarians in love will attest!

The fact that Aquarius is a fixed astrological sign can often lead to minor explosions, but when both partners are Aquarians, the problem all but disappears. Why? Because their stubborn streaks are more likely to mesh than clash. Aquarians are fixed about the same issues—such as equality and justice for all. Why would they bump heads? They agree!

Air signs can have trouble coming back to Earth, so care must be taken when it comes to life's little practicalities. But love conquers all—including mundane daily chores. For two Aquarians in love, that could be the best news of all.

Aquarius Woman/ Pisces Man

Because she's intellectually oriented and curious, the Aquarius woman tends to enjoy the sensation of being drawn in to another's mysterious world. In fact, intrigue is often the passport to her heart. And chances are excellent that she will be thoroughly fascinated by the zodiac's favorite Fish.

The Pisces man is a poet by nature. He swims in the depths of emotion and possesses an innate, uncanny understanding of life's mysteries. He tends to be a romantic, and his sensual, watery nature leads him to be gentle and unselfish in love—just what the Aquarius woman is typically looking for.

Because he is changeable, dreamy, and otherwise otherworldly, he inspires the imagination of the typical Aquarius woman. She appreciates his strange combination of wisdom and elusiveness, not unlike her own. She enjoys being romantically bewitched—and he's just the guy to do it.

But there are two predictable problems:

First, the Pisces man tends to be both dependent and indecisive. And second, he has a tendency to be oversensitive. If hurt by his Water Bearer mate, the Fish can spiral into a depressed state—the antithesis of Aquarian woman's natural optimism.

She may feel threatened by his moods. Are they contagious? If she decides they are, or if he makes too many emotional demands, the female Water Bearer is likely to reconsider. Maybe he's not as seductive as she first thought …

The Pisces man should watch for signs

of detachment in his Aquarius mate. If she seems farther and farther away, it's time for him to overcome his Piscean insecurity. Can he? That is up to the individual Fish.

But the female Water Bearer is usually worth the trouble it takes to keep her! And as long as she feels unencumbered, she tends to remain steadfast in her love. Such is the paradox of the Aquarian woman!

Airy Aquarius Woman

SUSAN B. ANTHONY
February 15, 1820–March 13, 1906

Driven by a desire to see both fairness and equality in evidence in everyday life, Aquarians (known as the humanitarians of the zodiac) often devote themselves to fighting for social change. And there's no better example of such altruism than the great crusader for women's rights, Susan B. Anthony.

Born in Massachusetts in 1820, Susan

B. Anthony learned about social awareness from her father, Daniel, who was both a practicing Quaker and an abolitionist. Intellectually and analytically gifted (like many Aquarians), she was reading and writing at age three.

She was initially trained for a career in teaching, but in 1852, her life took a different path. An outspoken critic of slavery, she worked tirelessly as an agent for the American Anti-Slavery Society in the years before the Civil War.

But she is most affectionately remembered as a pioneer advocate for women's rights. With her friends Elizabeth Cady Stanton and Amelia Bloomer, Susan B. Anthony vigorously campaigned against every aspect of the oppression of women—even the restrictive clothing they were expected to wear. Her courageous efforts to secure voting rights and equal pay for women spanned five decades.

Overcoming criticism and even arrest, she helped form the National American Woman Suffrage Association—and then took her show on the road, lecturing extensively throughout the American West.

She died before women secured the

right to vote in 1920, but Susan B. Anthony is everywhere acknowledged for her crucial and enormous contributions. In fact, the constitutional amendment that secured voting rights for women is often called the Anthony Amendment.

Susan B. Anthony never married. It is said that Aquarians love mankind more than they love any one man. This is certainly true of Susan B. Anthony, whose life and work have impacted every woman in America—and probably the world.